Why is the Human
on Earth?

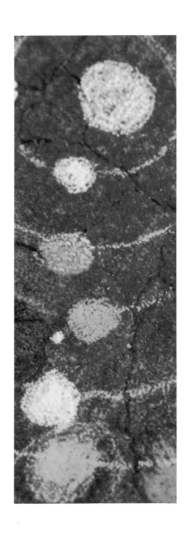

Why is the Human on Earth?

Working contemplations, to rediscover
— even for a moment —
the awe and meaning
of being human

Mark Ballabon

E P L

Eminent Productions Ltd
www.epl-uk.com

By the same author:
A Short Journey Of Poem Spirals
A Second Chance At Life

Design and layout:
The Flying Fish Studios Ltd
www.the-flying-fish.com

Original artwork and photography:
Jackie Henshall
Viv Mullett
Chris Ake
Mark Ballabon

With great appreciation to the editorial team of
Janet Donovan, Nick Ross and Viv Mullett

Printed in China 2008 by C & C Offset Printing Co. Ltd
on recyclable paper made from wood grown in sustainable forests.

ISBN: 978-0-9559487-0-1

Published by
Eminent Productions Ltd (EPL)
1 Bath Place, Barnet, Herts EN5 5XE

Why are the most simple questions
the most vital?

Acknowledgement

I would like to give the fullest acknowledgement to Leo and Ruth Armin and Ethra McKay, whose living experience of life and whose wisdoms and generosity have had the most profound positive effect on me, above anyone I have ever met in my life.

In which this book is part of a sentiment returned to them, for the freedom discovered in myself, to be myself.

And a mark of appreciation to my wife and friends who have supported and inspired me to take this all the way.

Dedication

This book is dedicated to all who burn with the quest to know themselves, and to discover and fulfil life from the depths of the unknown.

It is dedicated to those who hold a profound care for human kind and its purposes; those who believe that we are at a totally pivotal moment in human evolution, and want to be responsive to the changes, now.

In which this book aims to offer a toolkit of insights, by way of contemplations, not answers – for they can only be found in oneself and between ourselves, through such a journey.

This dedication therefore is meant as an invitation and encouragement in your own personal development, towards meaningful change in times that are so urgent for it.

Contents

The Quietening

The Journey of the Seven Contemplations

The Quietening

The person who perceives deeply why the human is on earth
makes a powerful release of knowing and respect,
for themselves, for other people, and for all life on this planet,
including the fundamental freedoms and purposes
that all people of the world have, and can share.

What wrote this book

AS THE COLOURFUL pieces of the puzzle for this book came together, so did three strong reasons for writing it – reasons that have continued to haunt and compel me in my own journey through this maze called living.

Firstly, I have always felt the need for a profound questioning of who and what we are as human beings, as a means to liberate much greater perception and a better response to the fact and gift of living.

And through this, to offer an oasis of easement and sanity in a world where often the primary drive – aggressive and blinkered – is for quick answers and solutions. In such a way, the very crucial questions that would actually lead to real solutions are rarely being asked at all. In which the question 'Why is the human on earth?' is probably the most crucial of all.

Secondly, I wanted to write something that might facilitate others to rediscover and touch their own extraordinary awe and passion and curiosity for living… not to write a comprehensive study about this, but to try to erect a few friendly and essential signposts.

The third reason lies in my wish to give some expression to the amazing and important natural patterns or templates by which growth happens in this universe. So these writings follow the pattern of seven – as seen in the spectrum or rainbow of light – which is harmonic and most natural to human development.

Therefore each chapter follows the gradient of this, one through seven; each chapter a step up and an attempt to climb higher and higher into the question itself.

For I have a great love of the human urge to refine.

"Listen to the silence,"
said the gardener to her friend,
"of the quiet space, inside of you,
with no need to pretend.

Resist the noise of 'I must have'
and find the ways that call
you to the beauty of yourself
that leaves you standing tall.

You are the finest instrument,
you, from mind to soul,
and oh, such tunes to play in life
that leave you feeling whole.

As long as you appreciate
that something mighty gives
that you can breathe your next breath in
that you in turn may give.

I've lived some years, but still know little
of why all came to be,
but to serve what gives such precious life
is reason fine for me.

So never lose the questing
and let them think we're fools
as we, eyes shining, rummage glad
in nature's box of tools.

Enigma, wonder, awe and care
light all the paths to truth
and electrify our will to live
to find out what we are."

Welcome into an increasingly bigger picture

please read slowly

WHY DOES YOUR heart beat an extraordinary 100,000 times a day? Whatever designed the vast 100,000 mile network of blood vessels in your body, or the 100 million light sensitive cells on the retina of your eye? What allows our brains to make so many thousands of calculations in a second whilst using only the same amount of power as a 10-watt light bulb?

Why do we have the amazing ability to distinguish over 4,000 different smells, or to see a star millions of miles away? And why in our galaxy are there 5 billion stars larger than our sun?

What is the majesty and depth and power of feelings that we have, and the astonishing miracle of birth, or the vigour of youth? What is the soul, and how is it different from the spirit? Why do we sometimes know something before it has happened? Why, if the entire history of the earth was represented in twenty-four hours, does the human only appear in the very last minute before midnight?

Have you ever really stopped then to ask yourself the question, 'Why is the human on earth?' This question cannot be wrapped up neatly and boxed under one heading such as science, religion or philosophy. It encompasses and integrates all of these, and much more.

It is a question that has driven, haunted and inspired people for thousands of years. The deeper you go, the greater the enigma. The greater the enigma, the more the quest to find out.

The more the quest, the more vital the question.

A teacher in Westchester, New York asked her class this very question and one 12-year-old girl wrote this:

"I believe that there is – despite the fact that we humans have caused so much damage to the world – a reason for our existence on this planet. I think we are here because the universe, with all its wonder and balance and logic, needs to be marvelled at, and we are the only species (to our knowledge) that has the ability to do so. We are the one species that does not simply accept what is around us, but asks why it is around us, and how it works. We are here because without us here to study it, the amazing complexity of the world would be wasted."

It sounds extraordinary and it is extraordinary yet true, that some children can know and articulate such insight and wisdom beyond their years.

It is significant how this nature of deep searching question is so pressing in many young children, and yet often seems to fade in later years as the raw spirit of enquiry gets overlaid by other questions, often of a much more mundane nature. Or sometimes a definite answer is come to, which then becomes a dogma, which simply oppresses the spirit of the quest to know.

If, in these critical times we are living through – where the mass pollution of toxic fumes, chemicals, perverse behaviour, diseases and sheer confusion and stress is choking us all – if the questions that are absolutely fundamental to the existence of life are not being asked, then we all suffocate on peripheral and trivial obsessions, abandoning and abdicating from the very purpose for which we exist.

And so to ask again, 'Why is the human on earth?'

What do you think?

Approaching
the contemplations

FROM A VERY early age many of us are taught to think in a 'beginning, middle, end' way. Some might remember science lessons at school where you had to write up everything under the headings, 'hypothesis, method, result, conclusion'. What this does is to engage brain logic – not the making of your own mind – which boxes and classifies and is always looking for the end result or bottom line, or the profit in things. These types of thought patterns can be useful in analysis for example, but in the bigger picture of human capability they are very limiting.

Yet often this nature of thought pattern is looking through our eyes when we read a book, and it leads us to want to get to the point as quickly as possible, or instantly define what the book is really about, what the conclusion is, and exactly how to classify it. In the case of this book, these pressures will not open up what is inside, or reveal anything at all.

The suggestion therefore is to try to *contemplate* what is being written.

Contemplation is a much more throughout searching and revealing process than just thinking, or even dwelling. And it involves not just 'front brain' hard calculations, but feelings, instincts, intuition, clairvoyance, curiosity and original ideas. It involves living in the now and being open to the unknown, and as uncomfortable as that may feel to our nervy, speedy brains, contemplation is a high state of real insight and vision.

So each chapter in this book is a contemplation in four integrated parts – a picture, a poem, a writing and a practical exercise. All four media together speak to the whole person.

Pictures, if you are open, activate the mind, mentality and imagination.

Poetry can release new feelings and new knowings.

Writings can engage all the human faculties into completely new understandings.

A practical exercise enables you to live it.

Please resist the urge to read too fast, sum it all up and box it without delay, however much this may irritate the brain's wish to get a result. It's not like that. When you think, you reference, reason and resolve. But when you contemplate you use the whole of your consciousness – all of your faculties, senses, intuitions – to connect with truth. To contemplate is to come home to yourself, to your purpose and to what you really want.

Do you know what you really want?

The Journey of the Seven Contemplations

Contemplation One

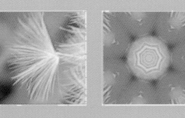
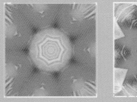

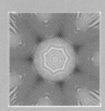

What shine is this
that warms my eyes
and fires my vision

What is this soaring feeling
throughout my soul
and restless spirit

Am I coming home
at last
to the thrill and promise
of life unveiled

Amazing, magic, charmed and graced
this life of many colours
with chance unending to be and do
beyond imagination

Lighthouse human
beacon free
behind your eyes
much more to see

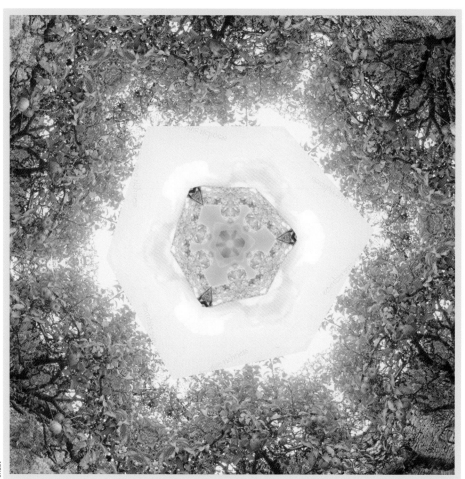

Peridot

To be in awe, and appreciate life for what it is

IF YOU LOOK into the tiny world of the nucleus of a cell, perhaps even one of your own, and gaze into those incredible spiralling chains of DNA upon which our whole physical make-up is held…

IF YOU LOOK into those astonishing swirling telescope pictures of the vast galaxy spirals, out there now, so far away that the distance is inconceivable – so bright, so light, so teeming with life it is unimaginable and unknown…

IF YOU TAKE a moment just to look at your hand and its intricate moving design and versatility and dexterity – absolutely not reproducible by any robot or all the computers in the world, now or ever…

IF YOU STOP to wonder how one tiny, tiny fertilised human egg, smaller than a dot on a page, could have turned into yourself, as you read this now…

When these things really stagger us, feelings of awe and wonder and reverence for life flow naturally and deeply, with the longing for it never to end. In which just to be yourself, and give of yourself, would be everything.

Then comes the clarity of mind, that we are – by design, by purpose, by the meaning of everything we can see, know, feel, touch – the highest evolving life on this earth; a human, with sublime capability to develop the intricate faculties that are gifted to us, from our minds to our intuition, from our feelings to our reasoning, from our language to our own personal character. Consciously.

The versatility is amazing. We can have a completely original idea, or compose music never heard before; we can experience touch, see close up and far away, use our instinct, our voice, feel the richness of passion, compassion, companionship; we can learn a new art, develop fine qualities to be proud of, in oneself, like courage, or care; be part of a team, appreciate a sunset, the shine of jewels, value another life, change willingly.

We can develop all our multiple human abilities, senses and qualities, ever finer, ever deeper, ever more successful – if we choose to.

It is a journey we were designed to make, becoming a true human, with being; where the discovery of natural ways and natural laws offers a true education, to connect to and free the real arts and skills and values that make us human beings, and not lesser.

The arts of true conversation, and not conflict or the competitive trading of facts.

The arts of listening, reflecting, weighing up, appraising, and not the heat and insecurity of having to have your say or force your point or pre-judge.

The arts of appreciation for what a thing is unto itself; for what the planet is unto herself; for what the sky, the earth, the fire, the water are unto themselves, and what the seasons are, each one unto itself; for what a cat, dog, insect, flower, is unto itself; for what a man is unto himself and for what a woman is unto herself. Each a unique part to play within the finely balanced web of life unfolding.

And to feel, as a warmth inside, for what this inter-connecting web of all is created to do, in harmony of purpose; respecting all life, for we are a part of all life, and we come from all life, and no part is separate. Only when we are not ourselves, when we become different to our essential nature, do we make destruction in the name of difference and cause separation.

We are in essence all of the same origin, for we are people, all people of human kind, in the template of our design, our purpose and cause. It is awesome, from the capability to look up and see Orion's stars in the night sky, to feeling your own pulse, like now, and wondering, what causes that… what causes that?

We are also unique, each one of us – our faces, our individual fingerprints, the irises in our eyes. Unique to find and choose our own way in life, in which difference should be the rich tapestry of expression, and never the source of conflict. For our expressions may be different, but our authority for living is the same.

The real struggle, the joy, the adventure and experience of offering the best of ourselves each day, not counting the cost, is how we begin to refine and develop what we are, and what we are here to do in life. This nurtures the appreciation inside that enables us to hold true values.

And appreciating life, our lives, is to wake up each day and be new with the new chance we have today, defying the cynicism that is there to disaffect us all; finding ourselves within the irrepressible quest of life, never, never looking back in regret.

To consciously live in this awe, this mysterious exploration and wonder about life… doesn't whatever caused humans to be, need to feel these feelings from us?

Is this therefore one of the first reasons why the human is on earth?

Exercises in Freedom
One

"Each day is new, live, open, ready.
Humans can be too
or they get claimed by the past"

Each day the birdsong sounds its new tune, the sun rises afresh, a new day awaits you. Nothing is yet written. But as this day starts, you can shift into automatic before you've even appreciated the new day you are in, or its freedoms.

Tomorrow, try getting up fifteen minutes earlier. Look out of your window or go outdoors. Take in the view for a few minutes, as if it were the first time you ever saw it. What do you notice that you didn't before?

Relax then, seated for a while, listen to yourself breathing deeply, slowly for a few breaths, and feel your pulse. Feel life coursing through you as if for the first time. What do these rhythms of life actually feel like? Stay with it awhile.

Then as the day unfolds, each situation you are in, each person you meet, look through your eyes as if it were for the very first time – which at that moment it in fact is. Be impersonal and let go of any instant judgements of good or bad, like or dislike.

For example, if you are walking in the street, or sitting on the train, look at different faces from time to time and simply wonder what longing or quality or hopes lie behind the face. You can do this with your own face in the mirror or with a photograph of yourself.

Try other examples through the day, other opportunities to look again at life, yours, other people's, the life of animals, the planet, water… as if it were for the very first time.

Lastly at night, before going to bed, think about yourself in a new light, impersonally, in terms of your appreciation of the beauty of being able to think or move, speak, touch, understand or feel feelings and the many extraordinary abilities that you as a human have been granted. Dwell on it, slowly. Perhaps write something to yourself about it in a special notebook.

This whole exercise, especially done often and developed over time, gives a release of freedom from yourself to yourself and to others, by not fixing them or you by previous experience, good or bad.

It helps develop greater vision by experiencing life less personally as a first principle, less revolving all the time around your personal opinions. And it may allow you to begin to rise above the habitual familiarity with life that narrows your experience of it down to a small corridor that only you can squeeze through.

So practice the art of looking and responding to life in a first time fresh way. You may begin to see and appreciate more than you believed possible. Remember, your eyes only see what you've taught them to see.

Contemplation Two

Life
the day and night,
the tearing and the resting,
joyful, sad
cutting, soft

Yet life
beyond the rise and fall
is the why and what
the where and when
and the who
we may become

Yes I am your great friend,
choice,
I lead you to yourself
I lead you higher

Choice
do no harm with me
and I will give you
your own freedom

To choose what kind of a person you want to be

WE ARE ALL gifted with the faculty of consciousness. It is what makes us unique above all other forms of life on this planet. And it delivers us the power of choice.

No self-determined change or development can ever happen in a person without exercising choice, consciously so.

In these fast-moving times, opinions and fashions shift rapidly, and one day experts tell us something is good for us, but tomorrow perhaps it's not so. We become inundated, from a very early age, with a need and pressure to make choices upon these shifting sands. And within the now very complex societies we live in, many of these choices are to do with physical appearances, identity and simply getting by in daily living, often to the point where making the deeper choices in life becomes a fraught, rushed or confusing dilemma.

Do we choose on the basis of everything and everyone else's pressures, or from our own position, our own experience, our own will? In which case, in the process of making choices, always motivating, urging, haunting and guiding the way ahead, will be the reason why.

As a first principle it is not what you choose, it's the reason why you choose it.

In the important things in your life, do you know why you make the choices you make?

Real, significant choice does not begin with facts, figures, pros and cons. At core, it is a matter of 'Know Thyself', which is a wisdom that has travelled to us over the millennia of human history, ever fresh and true today.

And one of the most important ways to begin this journey is through the ongoing choice and growth of your own standards. This is not a morality, it's a choice. Standards are the self-chosen values we stand upon, without which we have no firm foundation to know what we actually stand for at all in this world.

The crucial, first reasoning to do here is: to know what you will have, and what you won't have, in the living of your life, and why. This is best done as a regular exercise of self-appraisal, made conscious, even written up to yourself. For example, if you 'will have' fairness in how you deal with other people, then why, and how will you develop this and monitor it consciously?

This is real personal development. It will also involve the deliberate surveying and selecting of qualities that you want to develop in you as part of who and what you are. Honesty, courage or patience, for example, are seeds of human calibre that need carefully nurturing, in the light of experience, trial and error and lack of prejudice. They are qualities that carry the hallmark of a human with being.

Not only can this journey lead to finding one's own personal standards, but also to an inner settlement and respect for self, 'home grown'. It is a first deliberate step in choosing what kind of person you want to be, whilst making known to yourself what you don't want to be.

From such foundations comes the greater freedom to discover the true nature of what you are and may become; the greater freedom to perceive the causes of life beyond the ordinary, beyond opinion. For standards and qualities are the roots of real freedom of choice. They make us true to self, not selfish.

Are we not on this earth to exercise choices wisely, between that which promotes life, growth, and the natural ways and order that we are born into, and that which does not? For we can choose to be a person who listens, tries, admits to mistakes, endures, discovers, refines… or we can choose a life summed up by guilt or regret for example, or self punishment for not being perfect, or a self centred life blind to the consideration of others.

It's our choice. It's our consequence, each moment.

We are what we accept, and what we reject. It makes us the kind of people we are.

Without choice we would be robots, but with it we can still make ourselves so. Perhaps the ultimate choice for humans is to either develop our lives humanly, or to allow ourselves to become inhuman. Such choices are already shaping our futures, and if they will lead to a greater future then they give us good reason to be on this earth.

Exercises in Freedom
Two

*"What is the name
you know yourself by?"*

It's unlikely you chose your name. It was given to you a long time ago, and many years have passed between the 'you' then and the 'you' now. So whatever your name is – from Alfred to Zoe – is what people call you, and what you call you, whether you like it or not. In certain civilisations, cultures and tribes, names carried great significance. Names had a reason behind them. Think of *Richard the Lionheart*, *The Lady with the Lamp* or even *Dances with Wolves*.

When you get up tomorrow morning, find a name to call yourself which represents a quality or a nature that you want to carry in yourself throughout the day. Perhaps the name of a quality you will really need, such as *Grace, Persistence, Grit, Stillness, Will*. (Some of these are already used as people's names, and once this was a very conscious thing to do.)

Or decide to name the nature in which you want to do things during the day, such as *Finesse, Determination, Willingness*. Or perhaps a few words that characterise how you want to proceed, serious or playful, such as *Good Spirits, New Hope, Brave Heart*.

So find the name you wish to call yourself, and refer to yourself by that name in your thinking when you want to at any time. And if you wish, ask some friends to call you that name for the day, or week or longer.

In certain situations you may specifically want to draw on the name you've chosen. For example at a time of great adversity you might say to yourself, *"I Courage, will not be weakened by this challenge."* Or in another circumstance, if you'd chosen the name Quiet, you might say, *"I Quiet, will not allow the noise and stress of this situation to spoil my effective response to it."*

Names are very significant and it is interesting that we mostly don't get to choose our own. So this is exercising your own freedom to choose, to name and to grow in yourself different qualities and natures, consciously. It's quite simple really and very natural to a process of developing, improving and naming your own character, and not the one that might have been put upon you.

Contemplation Three

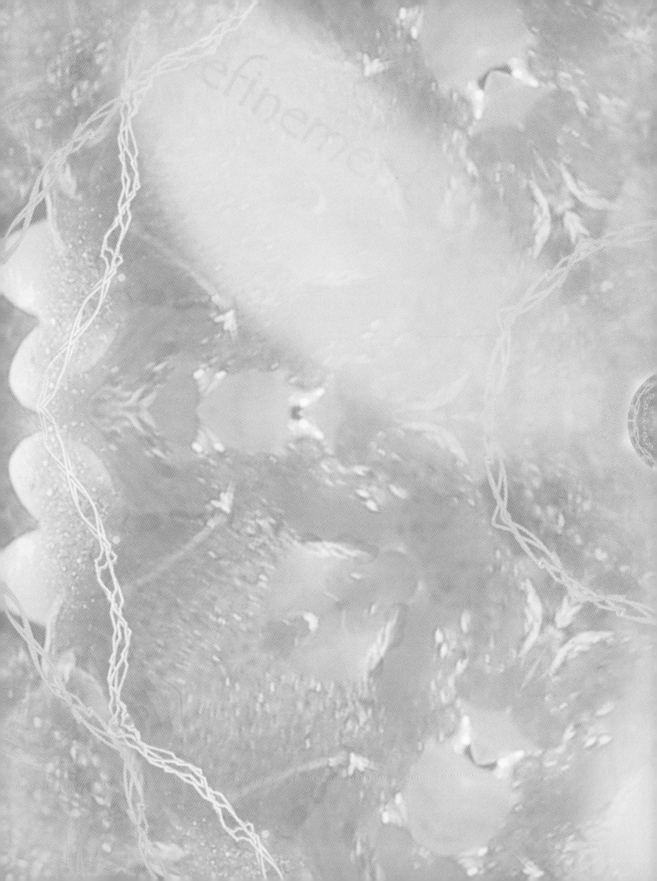

Looking up at the tree
reaching strong and tall,
and with vision,
seeing through its branches,
the sun
and the skies

Far beyond now
the stars and the heavens,
the cause and the reason,
where time and distance
hold no measure at all.

Do you –
in the hunger
of your longing,
and the seeking
of your soul –
not wonder
really wonder,
what magnificent, vast,
amazing whole
you are a tiny part of?

To know and feel a connected part of the weave of all life

BEING BORN INTO the world today is like being thrust straight onto an express train that rarely ever stops for you to get off, or change. And before you know it you turn around, perhaps at middle age, and find the thin thread of your life burnt at both ends, with many of your hopes and passions and aspirations unrealised.

The sheer speed of this and the heat of it and the stress of somehow not becoming the role model that everyone feels they ought to be, can squeeze us to the outside of ourselves – leaving us struggling to feel inside any of the thrill or excitement or wonder of simply being alive.

This profound malaise and depression, which seems to affect so many, causes in the end a whole reduction of living into the mostly petty, sensational, trivial side issues. Then comes the bottom lining, the pigeon-holing and the wholesale breaking down of how we view our own lives and the world, into totally disconnected little boxes of opinions.

A greater trap then looms if we end up thinking that the crucial issues of living can be dealt with and solved in isolation, out of the context of why the human exists in an infinite, integrated and virtually unexplored universe.

It's like trying to cure a disease within the vast inter-connected human system that we are, by believing that micro tests and results in the laboratory can always be effective in treating the whole person. This ignores the huge effect of that person's thinking and their stresses and feelings and behaviour upon their own bodies – even each cell.

Everything, everything in the natural worlds is an integrated part of the whole, by design. It sounds so simple doesn't it? Even simplistic. Yet it's so importantly true. And today there are scientifically proven researches that show that humans are made up of stardust in terms of basic elements found in both stars and humans. Well of course, of course, we are on earth, but we live inside a whole universe and contain its ingredients in us.

And in this universe, everything has a part, and is connected to a part of the whole, in which the human common perception of distance, time and isolation does not apply.

Doesn't the simple blade of grass at your feet not respond in its way, like you do in yours, to light and energy coming from the sunlight originating from millions of miles away? Doesn't your eyesight stretch from being able to see a tree a metre away in one second, to seeing a far, far distant star in the next? All are part of the weave of life, all inter-dependent, connected.

To be aware of this is one big step, to know it another, but to truly feel your existence to be one very small part of the whole is to make the biggest step of all.

The classic poetry that tries to describe, often with great beauty, the wonder of looking up at the bright stars on a dark night, seeks to convey this integration; but sometimes it can miss that last vital piece of the puzzle, which is that when you look at those stars, to know and feel that you are actually created of the same stuff. Only in the clever, calculated and sophisticated brainy thinking that we are all mostly cultured into, do we see ourselves as something totally separate, isolated, alone.

We live in an age of specialists, but specialisation can only ever work as a part of the whole. A practitioner can specialise in liver function as an example, but the liver can only ever really be understood in the context of every other living system and organ and faculty that is the human being, which it is connected to.

As a child, when we found the round peg that goes in the round hole, when we observed how the cat picks up the scent of a mouse and goes for it, when we looked forward to the summertime coming round again and again each year, when we played all day on the beach running our fingers through the sand and the water, we were close to, and sometimes inside of, this whole pulsing network of life where everything has a place, a purpose and a space to be.

So much conflict in the world originates from the wrong perception of difference: different colour, different creed, different nature, different way, different style. But these differences are the natural variety, beauty and celebration of life itself. And if we are at difference with the very planet we live on, with the animals, or with the trees, at difference with the value of our time on earth, and with each other and ourselves especially, then we begin to foment a civil war inside of ourselves; out from which we can only blindly see difference as a threat, an antagonism, something to be destroyed rather than upheld and celebrated.

Again, to be aware of this is the first awakening. To know it, comes through the great freedom and scope of experience and learning that life gives us the privilege to grow from. To feel it, is to be in the freedom that one gives oneself not to prevent the flow of it.

On this earth only the human can consciously hold this awareness and feeling, and respond from it, which is to gather forces together in oneself – ideas, discoveries, senses and ways that integrate, not alienate. In which the encouragement of others, the giving to and inspiring of others, the not putting down of others, is to free oneself to play an important part in the greater family of all humans.

Yet you go shopping in the local store, and mostly everyone walks around like they are not connected to, or part of the same human race at all, or the same purpose – we rarely look at each other like that. But are we not alive to be together, in the discovery of life, or were we all created for totally different reasons?

Isn't the human on earth to take up the finest part of one's choosing, to help in some way this whole amazing web of life to strengthen, to grow, to evolve? For without this conscious and mostly hard-won endeavour, which inspires good camaraderie, we are all alone and divided, especially within ourselves.

Exercises in Freedom Three

*"True harmony for the human
is a presence of mind
that makes the team that you are
play for each other"*

A wistful look at life may make you smile and simply say, 'Well some days are better than others!' And people tend to weather the storms to savour the triumphs. But the truth is that these are merely two imposters. For the seemingly endless highs and lows are all part of the adventurous, natural processes of learning, experience and the deliberate growth of wisdom.

However, one of the reasons we often repeat mistakes and don't learn from them is that we'd prefer to suppress the accompanying uncomfortability and sense of failure – rather than stopping for a moment to understand, appreciate, and move on.

So at the end of some days (that are worse than others!) you may find yourself tired, stressed, concerned and dispersed. And then you go to bed. Well, taking all this into sleep is not a good idea; and although the process of dreaming is in part to exhaust this debris, it is far better to tidy your mind before sleep like you might tidy up the kitchen or front room before bedtime, because you don't want to wake up to a mess. And remember the first exercise? Looking at life afresh, with a clear mind, is much easier without yesterday's excess baggage in your head.

Last thing at night and first thing in the morning are two crucial and very determining points in your day – if you want to be self-determined. And this exercise here is one to do before sleep. So give yourself a little time and space on your own to:

Sit quietly, and deliberately monitor your breathing and speeds. If these are too fast, then simply try to slow down a little. Even moving your hands in slow motion can help in this.

Feel the tensions in your face, across your shoulders and stomach area in particular. If these are too tense then deliberately try to relax them.

Think about the day you've experienced in an impersonal and non-reactive way.

If you have lingering concerns, find a way to quieten these, or reason them to a point where you could progress them tomorrow. Or if possible, simply relegate them, let them go.

If there have been special moments, learnings or important experiences from the day, make a real note to yourself of the significance of these.

At this point you may wish to write something to yourself, in your special notebook, about this process or about some new thought or idea that you want to pursue the next day.

Breathe in and out more deeply.

If you have a little more time, find a special small writing or poem or picture that has a peaceful, settling or enhancing quality to it. Meditate on it for a while.

You may wish to compose something yourself that prepares you now for sleep – perhaps a writing like this:

As surely as I feel the beauty
of my inner lives
and the easement of stillness,
so shall I now place my trust in this special time of sleep
respecting that which places its trust in me
that I may now be refreshed and made new
whilst I sleep.
So to awake
in the panorama
of everything being possible.

At a deliberately slow speed get into bed and close your eyes.

Sleep well.

Contemplation Four

The light softened
the talk eased
the pain of trying to be something else
retreated

We sat and looked
at each other
softly, kindly
through the eyes of no difference
and a longing for peace of mind

One woman, one man
many worlds to discover
many thoughts to feel
many hurts and wonders
to understand

And suddenly
the stillness shone
a ruby light
upon a jewel of knowing
that we could heal each other's worry
and preying pain
simply through the gift
we gave each other
of listening.

Ruby

To contribute
and add to life

SOMETHING INVESTED HUGELY in the creation of the human design, in every fine detail, every one of the millions of inter-connected working parts.

Not created from some great laboratory in the sky, but from a powerful consciousness of some kind, and a profound love of some kind, similar perhaps in small to how we feel when we feel love.

Whatever causes human life gives and continues to give. Everything that is granted life is given everything needed to survive, from a bee to a human. Giving is part of human nature, and in itself is a most natural act and art.

In these times we are living through however, giving often carries conditions, strings, 'should do', 'ought to', moralising, ulterior motives, politics and gaining control. With any of these attachments, giving is no longer giving, but an artificial act divorced from human purpose, compromising both the giver and receiver in their integrity and freedom.

True giving has no conditions, ever.

When you think about the child who rushes out on the cold winter mornings to feed the birds, in delight, to give freely; when you think of the couple who visit their elderly neighbour each week, to give easement, just because they care; when you think of the mother who goes to the local park, to clear the broken glass, because she doesn't want the children who play there to cut themselves…

Acts like these, not done for personal acclaim, not done from any cultural morality, but done quietly, when no one watches, because they want to. This is response to life, done consciously so, from the love of it, from the wish to help things on. It con-tributes, for it makes tribute to the beautiful fact that we have been given life, to give from it, in our own way.

To contribute is to express the very essence of being human. It is a powerful will and passion and drive to give something back for the gift of living. It is a personal religion, which in its seeking can release a whole theatre of rich dealings between people. Out from this comes the marvellous interplay and variety of human exchange, dialogue, relationships – a person to themselves and to friends, to strangers, to all living things.

When you can respond usefully to the unspoken need of someone in trouble, or ease the suffering of pain in another, you can feel the warmth inside that the release of giving gives back.

We are all living players in the expression of life, and each can contribute to it, without counting the cost, or measuring, or comparing. In this way it is clean.

We all know how hard it is in daily living to feel clean. It's really not easy because humans over the centuries, and in our generation, have often tended to taint what is clean and deride what is decent. And the way that this is done these days is to abuse life by interfering with or dismissing the natural ways and orders and needs of living things. This begins in humans and wounds the world we live in. Fish, as one of too many examples, were not designed to breathe in our sewage and toxic waste in their waters. It simply destroys them.

It is hard to conceive that whatever great architect caused and designed the human would want it to spend most of its life focusing its marvellous mind and fine senses into a computer screen by day and a television screen by night, living in cramped boxed rooms, walking streets in fear, bombarded by advertising messages, under constant stress, breathing in the poisonous fumes of cars as they pass by.

A lot of what is produced today – the vast range of consumer products – often take away, destruct or pollute more than they actually contribute either to humanity or to the planet we live on. So many artificial and superficial wants are created and often forced upon us, that it seems we must think today that it's impossible to enjoy ourselves without sitting passive in front of some screen, or having some latest gadget, newest fashion, current cool opinion. Yet somehow, at particular times in our history, before the addiction to machines, there was more enjoyment, satisfaction, even peace of mind to be found, say in the great art of conversation or discovering the natural worlds.

What is 21st century progress? And is something really progress if it takes away more than it gives?

Technology is not right or wrong, it's a question of 'for what reason and purpose?' For in this modern world of short termism, latest trends rule the day, with the compulsion of 'must have this, worry about it later', whereas clearly absolutely nothing in the natural worlds works this way. All the sensitive eco-systems on this planet have evolved interdependently, contributory each to each other, over millions of years. Yet these are being destroyed every minute, with little or no thought about consequence; it's mostly 'take first', not worrying about giving back. Meanwhile the natural worlds give and receive with fair measure, unconditionally, all the time.

To contribute to life, from a love of life, in the will to live, is a great liberation, and is uplifting because there is no weight of demand, no assumption, no greed.

A farmer can husband the land and the animals according to the nature of what they are, and the nature of what they need, in balance with the human need of what they can produce. This is done through the natural ecology that the land and the seasons provide. But if the sole motivation is commerce, then the soil is a commodity, the animals are a commodity, the seasons are marketing opportunities, all of which can render the farmer himself or herself to be no more than a commodity too – all is disconnected, purposeless beyond profit.

The purpose of human life is never realised at the expense of everything else.

To contribute is to live and to enhance life, because of the way you live it, because you feel connected to the world you are born into, connected to the human tribe you are born into, connected to this extraordinary universe we are born into, simply wanting to do your best for it – not to interfere with it, but to help it on.

This is a tribute, for it is a natural response to being granted an existence. It is the true human deal for us all, wherein we join evolution, not just analyse it 'out there'.

Exercises in Freedom
Four

"Giving a gift
is a well being science,
when you find what another person really needs
not what you think they need"

A young man sat up in his hospital bed to greet his brother who'd come to visit him that morning. "Look I got you some delicious grapes," his brother said, "that'll cheer you up," whereupon he promptly ate half the bunch and left a few minutes later(!) whilst the young man sighed inside – he didn't even like grapes…

In the afternoon his sister came in and asked him how he was feeling and if there was anything he needed. They talked quietly until early evening when the ward closed.

When she visited the next day she was amazed to see her brother up and walking around the ward. "How come you're so well today?" she asked. "Well yesterday you gave me the greatest gift of all, something I really needed." She smiled and asked him what that was. He smiled back and said, "Your time. You gave me your time, completely. You were with me, listened to me and made me feel valued."

So… think of a person or a group that you really value or respect – perhaps a partner, a friend, someone at work, or a charity, or organisation. What do they actually need? Could you give some of your time for them; or a useful present?

If you decide to gift your time, then you can do it by volunteering help or support or friendship in some way. Or you could find a gift of something that they might really need or find useful or enjoyable. But do research what their need actually is. This is a way to gift the preciousness of your time effectively, for in giving your time in the research, you listen and open yourself to what their need actually is. You are thus much more likely to find or do something that will truly mean a lot to them.

And before you make the act of giving, ask yourself why you are doing it – even if it's simply because you feel like it. For your reason gives great value to a gift, far beyond what the gift is worth.

Giving is an art, a skill, a freedom that can be won both ways. It is an endearment that is natural between humans who don't want to possess life or things or each other.

Care to try this?

Contemplation Five

"Yes, the way ahead is indeed blocked," she said
so wistfully, so disarmingly,
that the weight of her words
just flew away, like brightly coloured kites
in a strong gust of wind.

"Yes, we cannot proceed," she emphasised
as if strangely about to break into song.

"But,
we can now go backward one step,
to go forward by two."

I was stunned, couldn't answer,
and tried to work out…
was this a concept of the Tao
or a principle of physics
or a new religious precept,
or was she just,
in one simple, fresh swipe of originality,
absolutely,
one hundred per cent
right?

To generate originally

WHAT IS THE reason you get up in the morning, or go to sleep at night?

At the closing of the day we all get tired – every day. We're designed that way. So then we must eventually go to sleep, and during those hours we place our trust in the fact that something takes care of us, replenishes us, compels us to rest, repair, recharge, then to awaken for a new day.

Why would something have caused it to be this way – repetitious each day – for what reason? For something very powerful causes an extraordinary regeneration in us, that we may generate.

This highlights three major 'wheels', spinning together, and around which our human lives revolve.

The first wheel is all that we use of ourselves which is ultimately EXPENDABLE: our body, brain, history; which like our thrills, worries and disappointments, are ultimately expendable. All these, like our material possessions, we cannot carry with us across the other end of life.

Inside of this is the second wheel, which is that which generates a MAINTENANCE to our lives: from our heartbeat, our breathing, the moment by moment replacement of cells, to our inner world of teeming response signals, impressions, sensations and feelings... an awesome mostly unseen world. We draw from this maintenance wheel to nurture and grow many human qualities, attitudes and behaviours that maintain an improving quality of life and enhancement; out from which is the potential further enhancement of our relationships with other humans.

Within this is the third wheel, which is CONSCIOUS self-leadership (custodial). It is what we as people can generate, originally, by choice, out from the vast potentialities of life that the other two wheels make possible and will uphold. It is the wheel therefore, of our greatest potential as human beings.

So what do we generate, consciously?

The most powerful generation that comes from a human being does not come first of all from what a person does, but from the reasons why a person does something.

We know and see this every day in life. We see people, for example, get up on stage to try to impress and be popular, and they mime and smile sweetly to some song, which doesn't cause much and is often instantly forgettable.

But then someone takes the stage because they are passionate about singing, they are inspired, and they sing from their real living experience, a special story. Their voice carries far, far into the feelings and longings of those listening, and what this generates can even lift the spirits of a whole nation, or inspire people all over the world for generations to come. It is original, and it creates something new that wasn't there before – which is the whole point.

To generate consciously is to find the seeds of a reason to want to in the first place, whether in the being or the doing or both; a reason that adds to life. Then to plant the seeds of this reason in the garden of where it will best grow, whether that be in listening with patience to a friend, thinking a unique idea, choreographing a new dance, or any of the infinite fields of deliberate expression that a human can generate into, originally from themselves.

In which the success of it is that this is what a person actually decides to be and wants to do, for a reason they believe in… providing it does no harm.

Then we meet the personal development in all this; in that if our lives are not to fall into the many pitfalls of the kind of repetitious, monotonous living that makes our lives stagnant and meaningless, then we need to come at what we do afresh each time, with a vitality of why we are doing it and what it could cause. This kind of repetition is absolutely 'good for the soul', for it develops the right kind of habits and honour and ways in living that cause breakthrough development rather than being stymied. For whatever has happened the previous night, the dew forms fresh and clean each morning. We too can be like the dew.

And where can this begin? Well with the fact that each morning we are given that fresh start, that fresh supply of energy and 'can do', which allows us to generate out from ourselves into the vast fields of opportunity that await us. So there, right there, first thing in the morning, is a prime moment to reflect on what we would want to achieve that day and why – perhaps with a small meditation, or a reminder to oneself about what one really believes in; perhaps a way to come at things a little differently today, with greater openness or finesse or curiosity.

We talk about 'my generation' or 'in our generation', and it is true that in each generation of humans there is a new and different range of possibilities in what can be achieved and built upon for the next generation. However, too many perceptions in our times have become conditioned by the hunger for instant self-gratification, and are thus short-term limiting. For when you think of the cathedral builders of the Middle Ages, you see people who were happy and willing to spend their whole lives building in their own generation, for what they knew would only be completed and used in the generations to come.

How much thinking today has real respect or consideration for the generations to come? For in these times we seem to just manufacture more and more for today – products, technologies, information – with greed for more, getting nowhere faster and faster, mostly for short-term personal comfortability, rarely stopping to consider why, or what the consequences are or what greater purpose it is serving, if any.

In which we are rapidly losing the ability to be original and creative from ourselves, relying more and more on the copycat generation of machines and an over dependence on the latest thing, new model or invention.

We have extraordinary arts of communication for example, yet the more we rely upon technology the less we seem to communicate. We are over-saturated with information, yet we seem to understand less and less, especially about ourselves. And all the while we now place dangerous dependency upon the planet's natural resources, her own lifeblood, whilst we use only a tiny percentage of our own natural resources.

What a human can be and what a human can do is the original developing of so many arts and qualities, so many new discoveries and understandings never had before, never even thought of before, never felt before.

After billions of years of evolution on this planet, is the design of a human being not utterly original? We have the finest technology and equipment inside of ourselves. For what can match the powerful diversity of the human mind, or the human emotion or the human ability to feel proud…

Weren't we humans created so we can be creative too – without doing harm?

Exercises in Freedom Five

"If you are too busy, and too fast,
you may just pass yourself by
without even noticing"

At times during the week, sit in a quiet space, alone. For a few minutes, run through the 'video' of your time that day, or yesterday, and try to find and note down those moments when you may have wasted time – and why you think it was a waste.

Perhaps you kept oversleeping but felt no better for it, or had an argument that was unnecessary, moments of anger which led nowhere, moments of feeling insecure for no good reason, times when you defended yourself when there was nothing to defend, times which dragged by lazily and boringly when a new idea could have been pursued, occasions when you rushed something to completion making mistakes en route which wasted more time, moments of feeling guilt, suppression, regret or jealousy which proved quite useless, depressing or simply trapped you in the past.

So… how much time and energy do you think was wasted? Think on it. This time and energy might have been invested in something that could have kept you interested, refreshed, moving forward in your purpose.

Now write a brief note to yourself explaining what this exercise caused you to see that you didn't see before.

Finish this note by writing out one thing, one new mindset, one project or one simple conscious act you could do or begin tomorrow, to put something better in place when one of those wasteful moments crops up again.

As one small example: if you are sitting in traffic, waiting in a queue, or in the departure lounge at an airport, or you simply have an hour or so to spare, think how you would want to use this time to best effect. You may decide to deliberately try to think through an issue, question or opportunity from a completely new perspective, or from how a friend or colleague might perceive it; thus releasing you into a much better understanding of the area you are looking at and how to best respond.

Putting pen to paper in this exercise is important, because as you write it, so you reflect back to yourself some of the truth of how you lead your life – and therefore how you can improve it by small efforts each day to effect real change for good; and in so doing help others, by exampleship, which is the best form of leadership of self and others.

Please do note to yourself however, that time off, unwinding, even allowing a certain harmless sloppiness and being out of sync, or doing nothing much at times, may not be a waste at all. It can create space, rest and new options. Also, we are not aiming to be perfect.

Your freedom in this exercise is won in the conversion of wasted, spare or stressful time into powerful ways of winning back more of your life and mission.

Contemplation Six

The cool, smooth opal
a glistening, charming firelight
in whites and pinks and vibrant greens
fizzing, swirling,
spiriting the mind
far into space and timeless travel

you drift
beyond the reach
of your brain, your habit
your over control

breathing in and out
the pure fresh air
of new perceptions
and the sweeping rush
of new feelings

light years you fly
in just an instant
to a beauty of knowing
in your opal mind's eye
touching a truth
so clear, sublime

that
you
can
light
your
own
darkness

Opal

To connect higher from self

IF WE DON'T grow and refine what we are, what's the point in living? And how are we going to do that if we can't make connection to those things in us, in life, which help us grow and refine – like our passions, our persistence and those spirited endeavours that release the brilliance in us.

In the pattern of our daily lives we have connections to so many things, often habitually so, to do with our work, our home, our relationships, our worries… and all the details of it, such as monitoring the energy bills, tackling a problem, planning a holiday or meeting. The brain calculations and follow-through actions we make in doing these things use a limited network of connections, whilst consuming most of our time and space.

But connection beyond the daily routine and necessities of living does not happen simply through the calculated and detailed planning that our brains can do – as brilliant and versatile as they undoubtedly are, way beyond what any computer will ever be. We do however have higher parts in us than our brains.

We have minds to make up, mentalities to develop, instincts to sensitise, feelings to move us, intuitions to follow. How much do we use or develop these? For all of these higher natural systems in us allow for a completely different level of connection, with vast possibilities for personal growth and enhancement. But first is the need to be open and interested in the fact and workings of these higher faculties that live in us.

Take the instinct for example. Where is it? What does it do? How do we access it?

Well there is an automatic instinct in us, very quick and efficient, which amongst other things, alerts us to danger. It can cause us to swerve away from a cat in the road in an instant, before we have thought about it, or even become conscious of it.

But there is also an instinct to be developed; the kind of instinct that can rise when you walk into a hotel lobby as an example, and you just get this instinctive feeling that something is wrong or something threatens – but there are no obvious signs that can be discerned at the point. Then you later discover that a serious accident took place at that very same spot the day before, and your instinct picked up on it – you listened to it.

Then take the example of when you're at home, and seemingly out of the blue you get the mental picture of the face of a friend, and then a second later the doorbell rings and it's them.

Or the example of when you are speaking to a person on the phone and you suddenly get a picture of exactly where they are sitting and what's in the room… and it turns out to be right in every detail.

These are all instincts that can be listened to, translated and further developed as a fine network of connections with which to understand and better respond in life.

Then there is the even finer network of connections made through contemplation, if you can slow down enough to deliberately, quietly, work in yourself to create a state of mind, beyond referencing or thinking. A state in which you contemplate, for example the significance of spirals – in galaxies, ammonites, and the cochlea of your own inner ear. Your mind opens into the real unknown of this, and you are lost and found in the search and research beyond what you already know.

Time passes timelessly, and suddenly a completely new perception drops in. A perception that begins to reveal a whole new significance to do with the natural templates of shapes and dimensions throughout the whole universe – the natural designs that turn up in nature in circles, pentagrams, hexagons, icosahedrons and… spirals.

The human mind and mentality are the most extraordinary, powerful and infinite instruments of higher connection, from self.

These faculties in us can clearly be developed, and these examples just paint a few strokes of colour upon what is an absolutely unending canvas and realm of great human possibilities. These possibilities are to do with the connections that we can make above the ordinary, above the mundane; sometimes even beyond ourselves and into the unknown of what is yet to be discovered and released within the vast potential that we are and the universe we live in. These capabilities are completely natural to our design as humans.

How are such things possible?

Well, these kinds of connections – openings through which we as people can grow and nourish and live at greater depth of purpose – begin in small but significant ways. In which openness is a key starter. Openness, and humility, about what we don't yet know or understand; openness to the capabilities that we haven't yet discovered in ourselves; openness to make mistakes, be honest, take a chance, forgive. Openness to do the work of what will be needed.

This can actually revive in us an innocence of a particular kind, an innocence that is willing to explore beyond the confines of one's fixing habits and restricting self-view. An innocence that began in our childhood and had no conditions, or apathy, or cynicism; innocence, in the clear plasma of which, imagination and a freedom of expression was released, perhaps made brittle later in life by disappointments and regrets.

During these times when we are evermore pressed into speed and rapidity of decision making, where our brains become over-heated by the overwhelming tidal wave and bombardment of stimuli and impressions and persuasions as to how we should be, it seems increasingly difficult to connect beyond these demands and pressures which so often fix us into habitual get-by living.

But over and above this, it is true that we are so much better than what our experience in life causes us to think and believe. Somehow when we are oppressed into low self esteem, as so often happens in the pressure cooker of modern societies, we develop all kinds of unnatural insecurities and needs that only manufactured products can satisfy, or so we are persuaded to believe.

Beyond this daily battle however, lies a quieter, slower, more sensitive state within ourselves, waiting to be touched, worked and liberated into usefulness; to connect and grow the finer senses and capabilities that every human being is charged with.

We have such extraordinary, high abilities as humans – from fine healing arts to the amazing power of the mind – and are they not there to be used for a greater purpose, within ourselves, and far beyond?

Are we here just for ourselves? Or because humans together can make networks of connections that don't exist anywhere else in this universe, and which catalyse its future.

Exercises in Freedom
Six

*"What vision awaits our seeing,
beyond our vision"*

On how many days of our lives do we hold a truly tangible view in our minds of ourselves as a human being, a tiny speck of power, living on a planet, spinning around in a solar system, on the edges of a galaxy, amongst countless galaxies, within an infinite universe? For this is part of a true vision of what the case actually is every moment. And one that our vision rarely sees.

It's like by analogy, viewing ourselves as merely swimming along in the narrow lanes of our local swimming pool, when the reality is that we are floating around in the middle of the massive Pacific Ocean all the time.

Now a human mind, with presence, loves nothing more than the undefined, unlimited dimensions of possibility, for these are its natural playing fields. So this is a higher connection exercise in which you need to instruct your brain to just slow down, relax, and give up its control freak tendency – at least for a while…!

When we were young, questions were the excitement and charming mystery of daily adventure. And your greater vision and thus greater connection to understanding can be inspired, encouraged and led by the art of questions. So here is an exercise of key questions:

Take your special notebook and begin to meditate in a quiet space, perhaps with some quiet music, and without interruption, on the following questions. Give yourself a few minutes to cast your mind into these questions, making notes to yourself as you wish.

What is your vision of this world in 100 years' time?
Write down the first things that come into your mind.

What do you actually hope to leave behind you when your life on this earth is completed?
Forget listing houses, cars, etc. The question is asking about things that last a lot longer than bricks or metal.

What does the world need now?
List five key needs and the reason why you see each one to be a real need.

Straight after this exercise, take some more time to ask yourself what you have discovered. Slowly read over what you wrote. What do you think?

Try the exercise again in seven days' time without referencing at all to what you wrote the first time. Then compare notes. Later, see if you can do the exercise with a friend or a group. Compare notes and new discoveries. Enjoy it, connect with it, grow with it.

We humans are minute points of light in a skyscape so vast and beyond our vision, that to even begin to appreciate it we need to switch on the eyes of our feelings, intuitions and greater spiritual vision.

Connection and illumination are not weekend workshops. They are the fruits of a person who walks the fields of their lives every day, constantly seeking amongst what they don't already know, to find new ways ahead.

If we were more in love with what we don't know, we would know so much more.

Contemplation Seven

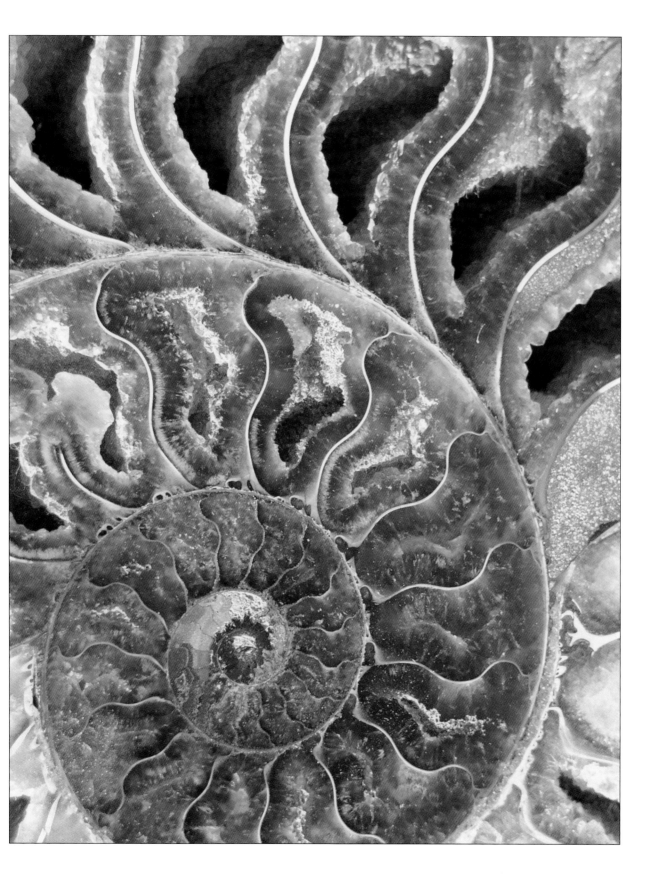

Aye let those sails fly full
with them crisp north winds a-whistling
as I peruse the latest charms
of that moon my dear old mistress

Soon the night will come
when those great high lords of light
will shine their starry signs
through my searching, sharp, far-seeing eyes

I be captain only here
to serve such lords and masters
as do move these very waves
and my hands to turn that fearless rudder

Sometimes when it's calm
do I feel such power pulsing
from heavens, to seas, into me
that makes my spirits rise in awe

Begone the pirate thoughts
that steal our very souls
making us believe
we're masters of this ocean

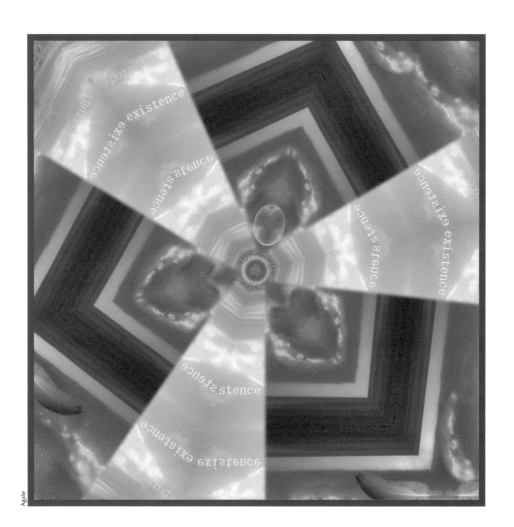

To understand
the natural government of life
to be free

W E DIDN'T CREATE life. We come into it, and are gifted it to live. And we live within a natural government of forces, seasons, time, space and the laws by which all our human systems naturally work. It was there before us.

This natural government and order exists at different levels throughout this universe, and across its infinite expanse it flows and evolves with great efficiency within the natural laws of its workings. But here on planet earth many try to oppose this, constructing their own authority, their own self-serving schemes and laws, against the natural grain of how life works. This makes us not free.

It is important therefore to begin to acknowledge and marvel at how natural government manifests. We are all compelled to learn to walk for example, to eat, drink, excrete, to go to sleep at some point, to express ourselves, because there is a government upon the human, and upon all life, which urges us to it, in our very best interests. These compulsions and urges are engraved in every human. They are a part of the marvellous order that upholds and cares for human life.

This fact alone negates the idea that the human lives in chaos or separate from any natural government; because we are clearly not free for example, to jump off the top of a mountain, or to fly to the sun, or to not eat – if we choose to continue to live. The evidences are everywhere, that everything we can do or think only happens within a natural government, there before us, there after.

This natural government originates in what can be called the 'unseen worlds' – the worlds of forces, energies, radiation – often undetectable by the crude instruments of machines, but very detectable by the fine tuned instrument that the human is. We live by these unseen worlds of electrical and magnetic impressions and signals – for what are thoughts and feelings and ideas actually made up of, or the signal that makes our own heart beat? And whilst we could maybe survive for a few weeks without food, and a few days without water, we would not last more than a few seconds without these electrical and magnetic signals and impressions – they govern our every move and all our senses by which we live.

So there is natural government for all life, mostly unseen in origin and seen in its manifestation.

And like any government it has its laws. But these are the natural laws, that give us day and night, the fine limitations in the human of hot and cold, the four seasons, the cycles of the moon, the rainbow, the human stages from youth to old age, the cycles of life and death; all of which are inescapable.

Every form of life is upheld by these natural laws, from the bird in flight, the fish breathing in the seas, the gemstones forming underground, the metamorphosis of the caterpillar, to the vastly intricate processes of human birth and development; from conception and the nine months of pregnancy to the onset of puberty and beyond – every living thing, whether in the skies, the seas, or on land. The natural laws sustain humans all the time, with each heartbeat and breath in every single person alive, whoever they may be. They carry absolutely no personal judgement, for they are part of the creational fabric of life, which allows life.

Natural laws make up the government that gives us the real freedom by which to live.

It is when the undeniable evidence of this is understood and appreciated that it becomes possible to work with and not against nature. For these natural laws are an awesome miracle of living, without which nothing could exist or hold to form. They are the so-called 'theory of everything', that is not a theory. Even the basics of science, and its acknowledgement of fundamental forces in this universe, attest to this natural order.

This sacred planet – absolutely unique in this whole galaxy as far as we know – is 93,000,000 miles from the sun, tilted at $23^1/_3$ degrees towards it, spinning at 1,000 miles per hour at the equator and orbiting the sun at an incredible speed of over 60,000 miles per hour. Think, really think and consider the extraordinary exactness and intricacies of this, over such huge distances, with supremely precise timings and balances, without which no life would exist here. Only in some kind of abstract, intellectual and self authorising, clever-clever thinking can this be termed chaotic or random – perhaps only a chaotic and random mind could reason so.

Yet from the moment a person loses the value and respect for this natural order – by not caring, or by believing their own personal authority to be supreme – the real destruction begins. For this is where a person pits themselves against the natural order of life, and ends up regarding living things as objects, commodities, to be manipulated, used up, engineered, for personal gain. This too makes a person not free, and possessed by that which they try to possess, whether a car, a house, a product or another person.

These basics are instinctively known by children, who often come to perceive very simply and accurately, that in the same way that you can't play with fire, you just can't cheat nature. And why would anyone want to? Except if they consider themselves superior to it, or not connected to it. Yet somehow, through the sophistication of intellectual brains, some so called cutting-edge thinking teaches that you can cheat nature, and manipulate it, engineer it, to the point where everything that is viable to do must automatically be valid as well – a truly fatal assumption. And so it is that our children in countries all over the world grow up with the worst pollution ever, many die from it, on a planet that is dramatically overheating, with extremes of climatic change, famine and disease that make for a wholly unsustainable future.

And could it be that something so simple, so obvious, as a child's perception that you cannot cheat nature, has been overridden by adult ambition and commerce and some twisted idea that all of this is progress, and technology alone is the panacea? The worst pollution is that this is being taught to so many children around the world.

Thousands of examples overwhelm us daily now. Each one tells the same story. Think of deforestation, and how this is destroying the natural balances of the very air we breathe, whilst also breaking up ancient tribes, families and taking away the beauty and wonder of wild landscapes of trees and starving the thousands of other species that depend on this whole ecology. Yet it continues to be done knowing this.

Only can this be rationalised by ignoring the long-term view of the continuance of the human race; at the same time ignoring that the forests are alive, the oceans are alive, ignoring their rights, so that they must instead conform to man-made 21st century laws and economic demands, whatever the consequence.

It is the same thinking that argues that the laws of nature can only be ratified through the microscope, telescope, in a particle accelerator or by some written formula, which dismisses what can be gleaned from a person's direct experience and research and feeling and detection. After all, there was a vast depth of knowledge that the Ancient Egyptians, Chaldeans, Babylonians and others discovered by detecting the natural laws at work, observing the heavens, the cycles and rhythms of life, using the instruments of their minds, their feelings and their living experiences. Now we see today just how accurate they were.

Deep inside, don't you feel that all life is inter-connected, and that one part can only be understood in the context of the whole?

There is more to be learned by turning the telescope of our minds and sensitivities upon the human, if we want to understand the universe it is made up of. Some technology of course, if used wisely, can help us into the future, but much diminishes the using and development of our own technology – our faculties and inner knowings. The ancient wisdom of 'As above so below', a true natural law, certainly didn't need a massive space telescope for ratification.

Many people already see with their own eyes how this planet's natural balances, climate and weather patterns are being destroyed by so many forms of industrial pollution. And when governments and nations are being categorically warned by hundreds of eminent climatologists that global warming is an absolutely undeniable, evidential and life endangering fact, and this is still largely ignored, then it tells us how numb the world has become to the appreciation of what truly governs all our lives.

We live in our homes, in our countries, on a planet in the outer reaches of an inconceivably huge galaxy, one galaxy amongst millions, spread over immense distances, beyond conception let alone measurement. The natural government of all this is an absolute wonder. It is not theoretical. It is alive and happening now. It is a whole universe which works, which functions brilliantly, integratedly, within an order, a natural government, way beyond the hand of human kind. And if that can't be respected and deeply appreciated, then we work against it, deny it, harm it and clearly ourselves too.

Our human experiences and feelings about the universe we live in cannot be dismissed as only a matter of subjectivity or sentimentality. The human is coded and designed to have feelings, and without them we would not even be able to register pain or joy, let alone the profound feelings of courage or reverence.

And when we look inside of the template of our own design, our complex organs, intricate nervous systems, vast brain functions and all the extraordinary micro integrated working parts, like the universe of the human eye, or the ear, or the immune system… is this natural order and what caused it and what governs it, not a marvel beyond words, to be revered, cherished?

It is the real, honest appreciation of this which again draws us closer to ourselves, in the seeking to be ourselves. Without it we are never free, but imprison ourselves in a world of our own invention, where we are not accountable to anything or anyone and we make ourselves alone. How can this be the reason why we are born on this earth, with other humans, made in the same design as us, breathing the same air, sharing the same planet and time and space and purpose?

Is the human not much, much more – a small, brilliant, uplifting part of this great, teeming with life, evolving universe, that is our true home?

Exercises in Freedom Seven

"Random is often used as a construct
to avoid the truth that all natural design
is precision absolute.
Thank God your heart does not work
randomly"

Life is not governed by our opinion of it. A cat, lightning, mountains are what they are. The way the blood flows, the lungs breathe, the rainbow forms up – they are what they are. And the truth of why humans are given life is what it is, no matter what anyone thinks about it.

Your choice is always whether you want to follow the natural flow and design of how life is, how it works and what its purposes are, or whether you want to create your own abstract idea of it.

This exercise is about discovering the amazing designs nature offers, including your design as a human and your freedom to develop within this design.

Go for a walk in a park or wood or by the sea. Find a leaf or twig or blossom or fruit of any tree that you are drawn to. Then search and collect a flower – providing it's allowed! Next, try to gather a few other things from nature that you may find on your walk, such as a feather, an acorn, a pebble, a shell.

When you get home – or in the park, café, wherever you can get a little space and time – place all the natural items in front of you, adding perhaps some other items you may already have at home such as a gemstone, a fossil, a plant…

Look at them really closely one at a time. Look at their shape, the pattern of their growth, their texture, the number of petals or sepals or lines or facets.

Then using your notebook, try to respond, through writing or drawing, to the following questions:

What are each of these natural items designed to do?

What governs their design?

What feelings do you have about these natural items?

Everything in nature has an exact design and an extraordinary in-built adaptability to its environment. But it is also governed by something greater than itself.

Everything in nature is templated to a purpose greater than itself.

So lastly in this exercise is the contemplation of what governs human life and your life. What powerful range of forces, energies, psychologies, habits, histories, attitudes and the influences of other people and events shapes our lives on earth?

So try to write down, in order of importance, your responses to the following two questions:

What really governs my life?

What really governs human life?

P.S. In a strange way, although we may not know each other, I feel that we have shared the journey of reading and experiencing this book together. For we are both humans, just trying to make some sense of the world that we find ourselves in.

And perhaps your hope and my hope and the hope of others is the same, and that the life we are all living, leads us in a mysterious and definite way, to set each other free.

I hope you will find as much enjoyment and fulfilment in travelling and re-travelling these pages, as I have had in the exploration. This book is not *the* journey or *the* way or *the* answer, but may be a very significant step forward – perhaps a change for good.

With respect, appreciation and endearment